IN THE PROCESS

Lisa C. Brooks

authorHOUSE

AuthorHouse™
1663 Liberty Drive
Bloomington, IN 47403
www.authorhouse.com
Phone: 1-800-839-8640

No part of this book may be reproduced, stored in a retrieval system, or transmitted by any means, electronic, mechanical, photocopying, recording, or otherwise, without written permission from the author.

© 2009 Lisa C. Brooks. All rights reserved.

No part of this book may be reproduced, stored in a retrieval system, or transmitted by any means without the written permission of the author.

First published by AuthorHouse 6/30/2009

ISBN: 978-1-4490-0225-1 (e)
ISBN: 978-1-4490-0224-4 (sc)

Printed in the United States of America
Bloomington, Indiana

This book is printed on acid-free paper.

Unless otherwise indicated, Bible quotations are taken from the KJV version of the Bible. Copyright © 1994 by Zondervan

IN THE PROCESS

Lisa C. Brooks

authorHOUSE®

AuthorHouse™
1663 Liberty Drive
Bloomington, IN 47403
www.authorhouse.com
Phone: 1-800-839-8640

No part of this book may be reproduced, stored in a retrieval system, or transmitted by any means, electronic, mechanical, photocopying, recording, or otherwise, without written permission from the author.

© 2009 Lisa C. Brooks. All rights reserved.

No part of this book may be reproduced, stored in a retrieval system, or transmitted by any means without the written permission of the author.

First published by AuthorHouse 6/30/2009

ISBN: 978-1-4490-0225-1 (e)
ISBN: 978-1-4490-0224-4 (sc)

Printed in the United States of America
Bloomington, Indiana

This book is printed on acid-free paper.

Unless otherwise indicated, Bible quotations are taken from the KJV version of the Bible. Copyright © 1994 by Zondervan

Contents

1	Where Did It All Begin?	1
2	The Seed	5
	a. No Regrets	6
	b. He's Still God	9
3	Going Through The Motions	15
4	Stay In Your Lane	19
5	Misplaced Focus	23
	a. Distractions	26
6	Don't Forget to Remember	31
7	Pressure	37
8	Don't Stop Dreaming	41
9	Friends	49
	a. Best Friends	52
10	Family	57
	a. They Are So Precious"	61
11	I Got This!	65
12	May I Help You?	69
13	Will I Ever Arrive?	77

Dedication

This publication is dedicated to my loving mother, Shirley A. Harris, a jewel in my life that I will forever miss until we're together again.

I would also like to acknowledge my husband, best friend, and the love of my life, my pastor, Michael A. Brooks. Thank you for supporting and loving me through this process. You are a true example of a man of God. Love you.

Ms. Darla Brooks; thank you for your time and expertise. Our long hours have finally paid off. Love you.

In addition, I want to thank my children and my church family, Restoration Fellowship Church International. Thank you all so much for your prayers. I cannot forget my three beautiful grandchildren D'shaun, London, and C.J. Nee Nee loves you guys a whole bunch!

Foreword

It's really not difficult at all to share my feelings about Lisa, for she is in truth, more kind, caring and genuine then most of the people I have encountered in my entire life. What you experience when you meet her is really her. She is a person who walks humbly with God while possessing an awesome empowerment to minister through song and word. Although I readily admit my bias, I too have been impacted by her character displayed in our marriage.

I find it quite interesting that many of us have a tendency to make snap judgments about people we meet. These judgments are usually made as a direct result of the affluence, influence, notoriety, position or celebrity of an individual. The problem with snap judgment is that you and I are without the ability to see beyond what we see in the moment. As such, our perception is more often than not formulated by our situations and not those of the individual we are attempting to figure out. I mentioned all of that to say, everybody has a story to tell of who they really are, how they became who they are, and what was the road that brought them. This book is the story of Lisa's who, how and what.

In my estimation one of the most powerful truths that you will realize in reading this offering is the revelation that one does not just show up out of no where, there is indeed a destiny ordained by God that you and I must walk. Lisa offers us tremendous insight into the understanding of walking the road chosen by God for your life. It is wonderful to know that we have purpose and destiny given to us by the Father, but it is equally exciting to know that we don't shoulder the responsibility to fulfill the purpose and walk in the destiny ourselves; the Father predetermined it and in his sovereign work the Holy Spirit is taking us through "The Process" to get there.

Michael A. Brooks

The Purpose

I encountered so many negative events in my life. During the time of each experience, I didn't realize that these confrontations were strategically designed by the enemy of my soul to destroy my purpose. Not understanding that God had great plans for me; I allowed some of these happenings to become issues in my life. What I didn't know was that God didn't consider my issues or incidents and judge me accordingly. Rather, He loved me unconditionally and His love kept me until I said yes to Him. I guess what I'm trying to convey to you is this; I know that you have faced conditions that made you wonder if you could face another day. Nevertheless, after the next day was there; you faced it! For that reason, you must understand that the same God that loved me, was loving you. If you allow Him, He will use all of the rejection and negativity that you had to deal with to develop the greatness He has placed inside of you. I pray that you will be inspired with each paragraph, and to see yourself as the righteousness of God in Jesus Christ. This is how He looks at you.

If you would've asked me two years ago, why are you writing a book? My answer would have been, "I don't know?" I started out writing a monthly letter of encouragement to the ladies in our local assembly, and the ladies on our mailing list for our women's ministry R.W.S. (Restored Women Sharing). I began realizing that God had placed something greater in me to strengthen these ladies. I had an urgency to share the love of God with them. The crazy part about the whole matter is this: when I didn't share, or when I didn't write letters, or send cards; I would be miserable. I was exactly like Paul:

> *"For though I preach the gospel, I have nothing to glory of: for necessity is laid upon me; yea, woe is unto me, if I preach not the Gospel."*
> *– (I Corinthians 9:16.)*

I do not have a choice. That's why you're reading this book right now. My prayer is that someone will read this publication and realize: "I can live again, it's not over, it's just beginning"!

The only way that one can appreciate the process that God has planned for them is to know the purpose. As you begin to read this book I want you to know that in each chapter, I've poured out my heart to you. I'm sharing my process with you because I want you to see your process as a road to your promise. Many of you on your way to your destiny will experience trials and tears as well as laughter and celebration. Remember it's all a part of the process.

A Process

When we think of restoration being a process, we consider time. The Webster's new world definition explains process as: a method of doing something, with all steps involved. There were several other definitions, but I chose this particular one because it communicates the move of God in ourselves as we yield to His word. As we are being restored there are steps involved and this is how we say it; "I'm going to the next level". These steps are evidence of growth, and the Lord's desire for us. He wants us to mature in our relationship with Him.

> *"But grow in grace, and in the knowledge of our Lord and Savior Jesus Christ. To Him be glory both now and forever. Amen."*
>
> *(II Peter 3:18)*

In addition, as we grow we proceed; yes, we advance, we come forth, and we blossom in this process. This is not an overnight formula. It took us years to make a mess of our lives and will take us a little time to straighten things out, but the first step in cleaning up is yielding to your process. Restoration is taking place in this development that involves many changes. Understand there will be times you don't know what's next on the agenda, but be encouraged in knowing that it's God's agenda for your life. He has a plan for you, and He will walk you through. That's why without faith we can never be restored; which takes us into the first chapter.

IN THE PROCESS

Chapter One
"Where Did It All Begin?"

**Wednesday
November 14, 1978
11:30 p.m.**

I'm sitting at the dinning room table with my sister, my mom, grandma on the piano, and a friend of the family was there; he was a minister. We were singing a song called, "I Walk With God", and I began to cry and be broken in my spirit. Being fourteen years of age at the time, I really didn't understand what was going on in my life. All that I remember is this; I would come home from school, go in my bedroom, and for hours I would read the bible. I would fast and pray for days. My mother would look at me and ask me was I okay. I knew in my heart there was more to God than a Sunday school class and a choir. I had a hunger for the Lord that was unreal. Not knowing that there was a void in my life and that this void was going to be filled this night. Well, to make a long story not as long, the Lord filled me with His spirit. When they picked me up off the floor, with tears streaming down my face and speaking in a language that I was totally unaware of; I knew the real meaning of being 'drunk in the spirit'. What a night. I got on the phone and it was midnight. I called everyone I could think of, saying…. "I've got the Holy Ghost!"

Lisa C. Brooks

I thought about Paul and Silas; and you know what, things <u>really</u> <u>do</u> happen <u>at</u> <u>midnight</u>.

I remember the saints saying, "I looked at my hands and they looked new", that is exactly what I was feeling the next morning. I started throwing clothes away, as well as some of my music. This was a new day, a new beginning for me. This was the beginning of sanctification and restoration. Believe me God gives us grace and faith, but we must sanctify ourselves through God's word.

> *"Sanctify them through thy truth: thy word is truth."*
> *(John 17:17)*

I realized, "wait a minute, I have the same hands, same feet, same face, and some of my thoughts were the same". That's when the Joel 2:25 process had begun. I didn't understand at that time, that with everyday of our lives, we are being restored. As we walk with the Lord He restores us.

> *"And I will restore to you the years that the locust hath eaten, the cankerworm, and the caterpillar, and the palmerworm, my great army which I sent among you."*
>
> *(Joel 2:25)*

God's desire for you is to give back to you every thing you lost. He has a double portion blessing for you, but if you don't change your mind, you will never receive it.

Just take a moment and picture a Father and son going for a walk in the park talking and sharing, as well as bonding.

In The Process

The son may have a few questions for Dad or maybe he just wants to be in his father's presence. That is exactly what we must do with our heavenly Father. Spend time with him. He wants fellowship, and as we spend time reading His word and praying, we are seeking Him. As we seek Him, we renew our minds. Yes, He gives us a new mind; old out, new in.

Here's an example: the old mind says, "I can never love or be loved because I didn't receive love as a child. I was abandoned and no one cared". The new mind in Christ says: "For God so loved the world that He gave His only Son, and that sacrifice was made for me! For that reason, I can love, and I am loved unconditionally".

A new mind is the beginning of the process of restoration, which allows us to comprehend that God wants us to have the best life. In St. John 10:10, it's called abundant life; the God life, complete in Him. Your process will begin in your mind.

We must have the mind of Christ. In order for us to develop a Christ-like mind, we have to renew our minds. It is then, that transformation will take place.

> *"And be not conformed to this world: but be ye transformed by the renewing of your mind, that ye may prove what is that good, and acceptable, and perfect will of God."*
>
> *(Romans 12:2)*

As my mind begins to change, which includes my soulish man, my intellect, the seat of my emotions will experience change. This is not an overnight method. It's not magic. It is

Lisa C. Brooks

surrender, then receiving, and finally applying on a daily basis. I surrender my will, I receive God's word, which is His will, and then I apply His word to my life. That means I become a doer of the word and not a hearer only. When we put this method into operation, manifestation will always follow. If you change your mind everything else will change. Let me warn you. This does not mean that you won't have crazy thoughts come across your mind or a flash from your past. The remedy for that:

> *"Casting down imaginations, and every high thing that exalteth itself against the knowledge of God, and bringing into captivity every thought to the obedience of Christ;"*
>
> *(II Corinthians 10:5)*

Chapter Two
"The Seed"

So often we read the word of God and of course we are encouraged, but when we find ourselves in the lines that we have read that can be difficult. For example, God spoke to the prophet Isaiah concerning His people being objects of His love and honored in His sight.

> *"When thou passest through the waters, I will be with thee; and through the rivers, they shall not overflow thee: when thou walkest through the fire, thou shalt not be burned; neither shall the flame kindle upon thee."*
>
> *(Isaiah 43:2)*

It's okay when I'm reading about the children of Israel, but what happens when my waters, rivers, and fires begin?

I'd like to share with you a part of my life that was very difficult for me. During this period, I was very miserable. I believe I was a young girl maybe twelve or thirteen years of age, and I didn't understand why my life wasn't going in the direction of perfect. You know, I didn't understand why I couldn't get new clothes and have all the things my friends at school had. Why did I go home to a house that was full of drug addicts and alcoholics? The only comfort I had was my mother. She always tried to make me feel better and she went to great measures to sacrifice for me, but at twelve, I'm saying, "why me"? This situation caused me to be depressed and suicidal. I didn't want to live. I didn't want to deal with the embarrassment any longer. I would ask myself why am I alive? So one day, I found some pills and I decided, forget it I'm going to end this misery. Then I could hear my mother saying "You know what happens to people that commit suicide? They go to hell". I thought about it long enough to change my mind. You know what? There was a seed in me and God's hand was on my life. Even though my father at the time did not know the Lord and my house was not a Christian home. My mother would make me go to Sunday school, not knowing that the word of God was being planted in my life. Every time I heard the word, I watered the seed and it began to grow. Yes, the seed saved my life and I didn't even know it. Stay in the word and water your seed.

"No Regrets"

On July 21, 2002 I lost my father. This was a great loss for me. You see, my dad, Charles Warren Harris was a great singer. He recorded with Motown Records in the 1960's, in a group called the "Monitors". He traveled the country performing in the Motown revue with many famous artists such as; The Temptations, Gladys Knight and the Pips, Stevie Wonder, and many others. Life in the fast lane was destruction for my father. We never had the proper relationship that a father and daughter should have. I do realize that everything we have is from God, and I believe that my talent came from my father. I really wanted my dad to witness the ministry that God placed in me through music, but it never happened. Consequently, dealing with his death brought me to a weak point in my life and in this time, I experienced God's strength as never before.

There were nights that I would lie in bed clutching my blanket sweating and praying that my mother was okay. I would listen to my father talk to this hero of mine as if she were trash. There was nothing that I could do but hope that she would open her bedroom door and come out of her room. Every time she would come out, I would exhale and call out to her, "Ma, are you okay?"

My mother was a warrior, she suffered a broken jaw and many more injuries, but it never stopped her from being an example to me. She never stopped loving me. What a great woman. I loved her so much for being so brave and I hated my father for being so callus. You see at the time, I didn't understand his issues; and to be honest, I didn't care. I had no knowledge that he was in bondage, under satanic influence. I didn't know that he was abused and neglected and introduced to sexual perversion as a small child. What was going on in my little mind was how "could someone abuse this sweet lady". He must be crazy. There were days that I hoped he would never come back home or that he would die in a car accident or be killed by one of his addict friends. I know that was really terrible for me to feel that way about my father at ten years of age, but that was how my life was rolling during that time.

I remember an incident that took place that I'll never forget. My father told my mom, myself, and my brother, *(a toddler at the time)*, this: "I'm going to the store and I'll be right back", my sister lived with my grandparents at the time. Well, he came back a month later. He called home from Mexico and had the nerve to bring back a sombrero! I was traumatized. Not knowing that he conducted a bad drug (cocaine) transaction and if found he would've been killed. My mother had to sell all of our furniture and our car. We had to leave our home and move in with my grandparents. I remember hearing my mother on the phone whispering, "Please don't kill him. I promise I'll get the money for you". I was exposed to this lifestyle for years. Coming home to a house filled with smoke, drugs, profanity, women, and loud music was normal for me. I must add this for the record. When my father wasn't drinking or using drugs, he was the nicest person on earth. He was very instrumental in teaching me how to be a manner able young lady. I had to say "yes sir, and yes mam". He had great potential but he was drawn away with his love for drugs and alcohol.

My father would prepare the cocaine in the kitchen and there would be mounds of marijuana sitting out on trays right at my fingertips. I guess you're wondering did I use? No, I never, touched any of it. It was disgusting to me to see people sniff this white substance up their noses while sometimes having a nosebleed. It was horrible to eyewitness men being thrown in a tub full of ice cold water hoping that they didn't overdose. I believe that I never engaged in the madness because God

In The Process

had a plan for my life and I chose to tell the Lord 'yes' at an early age. I didn't say I was perfect, but I did avoid a lot of unnecessary grief.

With this type of encounter at such an early age, I knew that I had to love my father in spite of what he put my mother through. Regardless of his monstrous behavior; if I wanted to please God, I had to love this man. Now that was a process! It involved much prayer and much time in consecration, but with God's help, I loved him more than ever before he died.

"He's Still God"

On Tuesday, March 16, 2003 at about 8:15 a.m., I went to McDonald's to get my mother some pancakes and bacon. Oh yes, and hash-brown's. She was persistent the day before and I was on a mission, not knowing that it was her last meal. Let me explain, my mother, Shirley Ann Harris was diagnosed with colon cancer in June of 2003. She was taking chemotherapy, and she was becoming progressively weaker with each passing day. This lady was always strong naturally as well as spiritually. You could always find her encouraging someone. It didn't matter who it was; could have been a stranger on the street or in the grocery store. She was either on the phone or in someone's face telling them, "you can make it, don't give up just trust God." She was on fire for the Lord, considering how she endured twenty plus years, in an abusive marriage relationship with my father. She would tell you without hesitation that God is good.

Seeing my mom in this state of sickness was the greatest challenge that I had ever faced in my life. I was actually experiencing my faith being tried in the fire. I had so many questions for God. I didn't understand this scenario; she was only 64 years old, never hospitalized for any severe illnesses, always full of energy and joy, and she loved being a child of God. My mom would tell me "Lisa, there's nothing too hard for God". For that reason, I believed that Shirley Harris would be around for a long time. For the entire eight months we prayed together, confessed the word of God together, cried together, and praised God together; but on March 17, 2004 at 12:15 a.m. she wanted to be with the Lord and I wanted her to stay with me.

It was as if I were dreaming. Please don't misunderstand me; I know she's in a better place; a place that's unimaginable, and a place that we all look forward to going to one day. She is already there and that is comforting to know, but it did not erase the pain that I was feeling that evening in the hospital waiting room. I felt like I was ten years old. I remember saying to myself, "I want my mama", at forty years of age. My daughters and my son were in the room with my mom as she was making her transition. I knew that I must trust God or I would not make it through this experience. LaTia began to sing her favorite song, "Anointing Fall On Me", while holding her hand, and continued, "Let the power of the Holy Ghost fall

In The Process

on me, anointing fall on me". Her heart began to race, and then it slowed down until she flat-lined with no cardiovascular activity left. I wanted someone to wake me up, but fortunately for her, I was not dreaming.

There were so many thoughts and images that raced through my mind, as my mother was expiring. I recalled the years I spent with her as a young child; the discipline she enforced, and the love that she poured into me for 40 years of her life. Then I began to put the puzzle together, she knew all this time that she wasn't going to be with us long. Now I could grasp why, days that I would visit with her in the hospital and nursing home, her fingers would have blood on them. This happened from her catching the blood trickling down her nose in the middle of a conversation. We would wash her hands and face wondering why does she have nosebleeds everyday? She didn't tell me; she had a tumor on her brain. My mother didn't want us to worry, and I believe that she was in denial. I can recall asking her, "Mother, exactly what are your doctors saying?" I noticed that she would never give me a direct answer, so I told her, "Please don't withhold any information from me, I love you and you are not a burden to me. You have been here for me all of my life, and now it's my turn". She would always say, "I know, but I'm okay. You know the doctors say a lot of things, but I don't receive it. I'm in the Lord's hands".

When I tell you this was a challenge for me, it was more than I expected. I was so aggravated. I knew that I clearly could not and would not call God Almighty on the carpet, but I asked myself was there anything different that I could have done? At this point, in the midst of tears, I had to control my thinking process with the word of God. I could stand on this truth: I honored my parents until the day that they both died; and honoring them is what was required of me by God.

> *"Honour thy father and thy mother: that thy days may be long upon the land which the Lord thy God giveth thee."*
>
> *(Exodus 20:12)*

I realized that I must stay yielded to the word of the Lord, not because this is what my mother would have wanted me to do; but it was what God expected for me to do. He wants me to totally depend on Him. When I don't understand, and when I'm weak and confused. That is when His strength and love is manifested.

No doubt this was a challenge for me and there were times that I felt like an orphan. My father passed in July of 2002 and now my mother. I called her my "sweetheart". Let me encourage you, maybe you have encountered this same situation and you feel as if you're loosing control. Remember this: we don't walk and live by our feelings, we live by faith and our objective is to build on our faith. Paul tells this in *Romans 10:17*

> *"So then faith cometh by hearing, and hearing by the word of God."*

I know that God does all things well and I realize that I must take one day at a time, trust the Lord, stay in His face, stay in His word, and continue to walk in purpose. I know that one day we will see our loved ones again; and what a great day! In the mean time, the signs of His sovereignty are ever present; they help me to stay focused and to realize that *He's still God!*

Chapter Three
"Going Through the Motions"

Shortly after my mother's death I would find myself going through the motions. I would basically deal with every day life out of habit with absolutely no enthusiasm. I was thinking about her all the time, and of course missing her like crazy. For a while, my emotions were numb, and I had a long list of questions on my mind with no answers. I held on to the truth of God's word.

> *"And we know that all things work together for good to them that love God, to them who are the called according to his purpose."*
>
> *(Romans 8:28)*

I knew that I was one of them, I mean there was no doubt that I loved God and I was positively sure that I was called by God and walking in His purpose for my life. I realized that I needed to stay humble before the Lord so that I could receive my healing. In case you're wondering, I still miss her and think about her everyday. Yet, the more I would cling to Him, His strength was becoming perfect in my weakness. There's nothing wrong with you when you have a broken experience. That's a wonderful position to be in to have God deal with you. While you're there, just remember that you don't have to stay there. He will increase your strength.

Lisa C. Brooks

> *"He giveth power to the faint; and to them that have no might he increaseth strength."*
>
> *(Isaiah 40:29)*

I was determined not to allow this time of grief and bereavement to overwhelm me. Consequently, I had to constantly remind myself that I was an over-comer, and that the greater one lived in me. During this period, I battled with so much guilt, punishing myself because I didn't feel the same level of excitement and enthusiasm. Neither did I operate with the momentum I was accustomed to.

Inevitably, I received great revelation from the spirit of God! You see the things that I was doing out of habit were the things of God. I was yet faithful to ministry, praying, studying, and doing those things that would advance the kingdom of God. Even though I did not <u>feel</u> like doing these things, I did them regardless; realizing that it is not a *feeling* walk, but it is a *faith* walk. The more that I released faith and continued to trust God, the more enthusiastic I became. Listen, whatever you do, never beat yourself up if you find yourself in the process and you don't feel in your flesh as though you are covering any ground. Just keep doing those thing that please God and He will strengthen you!

The matter at hand is that your labor of love will never be in vain. Remember this:

> *"For as the body without the spirit is dead, so faith without works is dead also."*
>
> *(James 2:26)*

In The Process

You may discover yourself in a position of pressing your way, but the key is to <u>keep</u> pressing. As you persevere in faith, you are not alone! Now I know there are circumstances that will arise in the process that will make you feel like no one is there for you. You may not understand it right now, but that's a good place to be in. As you continue to press you will appreciate this time. You must recall the words of our Lord and Savior!

> *"Teaching them to observe all things whatsoever I have commanded you: and, lo, I am with you always, even unto the end of the world. Amen."*
> *(Matthew 28:20)*

Chapter Four
"Stay in Your Lane"

"Only be thou strong and very courageous, that thou mayest observe to do according to all the law, which Moses my servant commanded thee: turn not from it to the right hand or to the left, that thou mayest prosper whithersoever thou goest."

(Joshua 1:7)

Let me ask you a question, do you know who you are? I am persuaded that this generation is suffering from a severe case of 'identity crisis', and if they don't embrace what God has said in His word concerning who they are and why they exist, they will <u>never</u> walk in purpose. This implies that one is existing but surprisingly doesn't know why. It is what we call whistling in the dark and going no where fast. The prophet Isaiah speaks to us in chapter 43:7:

"Even every one that is called by my name: for I have created him for my glory, I have formed him; yea, I have made him."

(Isaiah 43:7)

This scripture explains to us that we were created by God, which actually means that you and I were shaped, formed, and brought into being to glorify God! Affirmatively, we must understand that God is all-powerful, and He is the God of creation (Elohim), and He does all things well! Consider yourself every time that you look in the mirror; you are looking at God's creation, and there is only one you. No one else has your DNA, no one can be you, and you can never become anyone else. Now if we know this to be true, why do people pay money to attempt to look like another individual? Some people find it necessary to alter what God has fashioned in the womb.

I believe that life can be so wonderful if we accept what God Has created and <u>stay in our lane</u>. My lane is my path, my course, my purpose, who I am, what God has placed in me, and everything God made me to be; since I can only be me! No doubt when I try to be someone that I'm not, I will only frustrate the process. God wants a return on His investment and we should give back to Him everything that He placed in us. Understand it is impossible for me to give to God what he has put in you, simply, because I'm not you. Therefore, if we honestly give it some thought, being jealous of someone else is out of the question. When I'm in my lane and you are in your lane, I am confident of my identity; I can celebrate who you are without competition or strife! When God looks at us He sees the righteousness of Jesus Christ! WOW! What a great sacrifice Jesus made for us so that we can be free and be everything that He put us on this earth to be. We have the audacity to be unsatisfied with our looks and our talents. Now that's a lot of nerve! My mind goes back to when I was a young girl and my friends and family use to tease me about my pointed nose. I mean they would call me names that I won't share with you, and I thought there was something wrong with me. I would tell my mother, "I must be adopted seeing that, I

In The Process

don't look like anyone in my family". As I became an adult, I realized, "Hey, this nose is kind of cute". I made the decision that I would just work with what God gave me and that is exactly what I encourage you to do. Work with what God has given you! After all, it's not that bad. When we band with God's process, we will love everything about ourselves. By virtue of God creating you; you can only be the best you.

When all of the odds were against Joshua, he remained steadfast in the Lord and He trusted His word. Joshua and Caleb were a minority among the twelve spies sent out by Moses to search the land of Canaan. Opposition and pressure from the majority did not interfere with their confidence in God.

> *"If the Lord delight in us, then He will bring us into this land, and give it us; a land which floweth with milk and honey."*
>
> *(Numbers 14:8)*

Search your surroundings. Now if you're not looking at your milk and honey that God promised you; if you have not possessed your land; maybe you need to get back in your lane, your position. That's were you're blessing is coming, and if you are not there when it gets there, you will never receive what God has for you.

Being a native Detroiter with a musical background, the Lord opened a major door for me to minister to the masses in April 1986. Michael A. Brooks, a founding member and writer as well as producer, of the group "Commissioned", formed a female singing group called Witness. When I received the phone call to be a part of this music ministry, I didn't know that

Lisa C. Brooks

the Lord had great plans for this group. I said yes, because I loved to sing.

At the time I was about 23 years of age and I spent 13 years singing with my family in a group called the "Voices of Eden", which consisted of my mother, my sister, and I. We would sing throughout the city of Detroit and we did a few local television programs. I remember one program called "Gospel Time". This was a wonderful experience for me. Basically it was preparing me for my purpose that I walk in today. It taught me how to use the talent that the Lord gave me and never measure myself to anyone else, but rather appreciate their talent, and perfect what you have to offer.

Detroit is a city that has singers and musicians on every corner which brings me to a comment that I usually get when I travel across the country. "Is it in the water?" Of course not, but it is imperative that you know your limitations and become excellent in your lane.

Your path has been prepared for you. It is not necessary to be inquisitive about what's going on in the lane next to you. Someone else's purpose, dream, and vision doesn't concern you. My opinion is this: If we don't enjoy the ride, love life, and do what is necessary to mature and become excellent in our lane; we will not ever appreciate the path that has been prepared for us.

Chapter Five
"Misplaced Focus"

What does it mean to focus? It is any center of attention. God must be the center of attention in our lives; when He is not, that's when we will find ourselves in trouble. There was a time in my life when there were just my three children, myself, and a raggedy BMW 320i. I was saved, I loved the Lord, faithful concerning the things of God, but I had one major problem; 'misplaced focus'. I was concerned more about my feelings, my stuff, and my world. You could say I was self consumed, focusing on my struggle, looking at my circumstances, as opposed to concentrating on my source and provider.

"For the Maker is thine Husband the Lord of hosts is his and thy Redeemer the Holy One of Israel; The God of the whole earth shall he be called."
(Isaiah 54:5)

Lisa C. Brooks

When we put God on the throne He becomes greater than any difficulty challenge, adversity, or trouble that we will ever face. Before we move on, we must ask ourselves this question: "Who is on the throne of my heart?" I knew that if I expected to survive I had to learn how to be alone, and know that God was concerned about me. He was there for me at all times. I had to become whole and complete in Him before I could move on to the next stage in my life.

> *"And ye are complete in him, which is the head of all principality and power:"*
>
> *(Colossians 2:10)*

Do yourself a favor. Find out what God has said about you in His word and make that the center of your attention. Trust me, when you do this there will be no room for impatience, inferiority, or low-self esteem. You must know who you are in Jesus Christ and remain steadfast in that. You may have to remind yourself and everyone else, of this, "I am the righteousness of God in Jesus Christ". It's okay because that is exactly who you are. Now in your process the worse thing that you can do to yourself is place emphasis on what man says or thinks about you. If you place any focus on that element, you will never go where God is trying to take you. God's promises and man's opinion will never mix.

> *"For my thoughts are not your thoughts, neither are your ways my ways, saith the Lord."*
>
> *(Isaiah 55:8)*

In The Process

Don't focus on what you see, focus on the word of God that you know. That's what makes you free! His word says:

> *"Faithful is He that calleth you, who also will do it."*
>
> *(I Thessalonians 5:24)*

Place your faith and focus in His promises. He has begun a good work in you and he will complete it! Do you know when the work started in you? The day you said 'yes' to the Lord. Maybe you're thinking, "Well since I've been a Christian, I've messed up several times". Regardless of the mistakes that you made, you were still in God's process; and His work in you was still working! When you have a heart for God you will always find yourself in His face asking Him for His grace. His grace will continue you on your path.

Misplaced focus will kill your dreams, aspirations, and eventually your vision. Remember that if God made you a promise, He always confirms His word with manifestation! Get your mind on who God is and keep it there for the rest of your life. Now that's focus!

Focus is radical when you truly get concentrated on seeking God. You will probably be perceived as off, weird, too deep, going to the extreme, or even fanatical to some people around you; and my answer for that; "SO WHAT!" Of course we know the natural man will always see the spiritual realm as foolish.

> *"But the natural man receiveth not the things of the Spirit of God: for they are foolishness unto*

> *him; Neither can he know them, because they are spiritually discerned."*
>
> *(I Corinthians 2:14)*

"Distractions"

Make no mistake about it; just when you have a hold on your life and you are moving forward at a steady focused pace something will come out of no where to frustrate you and get your attention. I call these uninvited pop-ups. <u>Distractions;</u> This is how Paul defines it:

> *"Ye did run well; who did hinder you that ye should not obey the truth?"*
>
> *(Galatians 5:7)*

There are times when we need to stop and ask ourselves, "What happened?" What person or circumstance caused me to veer out of and away from my process? What was the thing that I allowed to draw my mind away from my goals and dreams and aspirations that I expected to take place in my life? It is easy to ask yourself these questions, but the difficult part comes into play when we answer the questions and realize that if I don't extract my self out of the equation; and if I am always placing my attention on the distractions,

In The Process

I will never experience true success. I used the term, 'true success' because I would always find myself in the start-stop mode, never completing anything, and therefore, never accomplishing God's desire for my life. God spoke these words to Joshua:

> *"This book of the law shall not depart out of thy mouth; but thou shalt meditate therein day and night, that thou mayest observe to do according to all that is written therein: for then thou shalt make thy way prosperous, and then thou shalt have good success."*
>
> *(Joshua 1:8)*

This scripture educates us on how to obtain success. That only comes in and through studying and obeying the word of God. Sometimes we give attention to these distractions, which cause us to perceive a situation that looks like a favorable outcome, when it is actually the opposite.

We must allow God's word to saturate our minds and by doing so; we will receive the wisdom, direction and strength to stand-fast on the word of the Lord. Remember that He that promised is faithful. We have to put on spiritual blinders so that we won't be distracted by what is going on around us, or what we see in the natural realm.

It is mandatory for the people of God to move full speed ahead in purpose. It's time for us to focus on what God has said to us in His word and stop concentrating on popular opinion, our logic or tradition. Understand the purpose for 'pop-ups' is that they come to slow you down and these eventually **control**

Lisa C. Brooks

your focus.

What happens when I do not concentrate on God's purpose for my life and I focus on the things that come to frustrate my expectations and aggravate my progress? At some point I will become discouraged and I will find myself in a state of doubt and unbelief. This is a terrible state, because I am no longer walking by faith; I am reacting to distractions!

I promised you at the inception of this writing that I was a straight forward individual and I must be authentic in my declaration okay? Listen, don't you think that we, (that means You and Me), have wasted enough time being in the will of God for our lives one year and then the next year out of the will; off of the course, not sure about the purpose? Come on! Enough is enough! It is time for us to stay focused and be blessed! He that endureth unto the end shall be saved. Isn't it crazy that we can be patient with individuals that have let us down over and over, but when it comes to taking God at His word, it isn't the same. If He doesn't show up at the time we expect Him to, we place our focus on what we think is the next best thing or person for satisfaction; only to find ourselves back at ground zero. It is time for us to stay with the Lord and continue to trust Him. If we don't see it, feel it, or think it, it does not matter. He said it, and we have a Father that honors His word. If we remain in the process, we will see that He does all things well. Think about it, you've said, "Yes Lord" all this time and your "Yes Lord" brought you to this place of maturity and strength in God. Therefore, why would you allow something to interfere with your momentum now?

Let me share with you a major diversion that took place

In The Process

in my life. It was the year 1981. I was a senior in high school. Not just an average student; I was singing in the Gospel choir, and very involved with the senior activities. I received a music scholarship at a university, but I didn't take advantage of that opportunity. I had no direction. My concern at the time was a passport out of my home. I wanted to get away from the environment, but I didn't want to leave my mother. As a result, I could not move away from Detroit because of how I felt. I had a need to be close to her. I can recall at one point living with my Uncle Mack and Aunt Joan for a short time. I was so grateful to them for allowing me to come into their home. It was a breath of fresh air. It was so peaceful and I enjoyed laughing and talking with my Uncle Mack from Greenwood, Mississippi. Boy, did he have some stories. My Aunt Joan was my mother's only sister. She was younger than my mom, and wasn't strict; it was great!

I enjoyed going to school, not to mention I graduated Cum Laude. Bear in mind what I shared with you of how my process actually started when I was 14 years old. What I didn't understand at 18 was this; maturity is a primary factor in the process. I considered my life as okay.

I attended a local college, and was on the Dean's list. I thought I wanted to major in criminal justice. Oh yes, I thought I had it all figured out, but what I didn't know was this; the devil had a plan for me. You see I wasn't prepared. As a immature Christian, I really didn't understand at the time that I had to be dressed properly or I wouldn't survive the attack from the enemy.

> *"Put on the whole armour of God, that ye may be able to stand against the wiles of the devil."*
>
> *(Ephesians 6:11)*

During this stage of incompleteness in my life, I conceived my first born child, Natasha Page. Yes, I was terrified and I was embarrassed. I didn't know how to face my mother, I didn't know how to tell my pastor, and all this was a big deal for me. You see, I had great respect for the man of God and I was so ashamed of myself. Here I am pregnant at 18, teaching Sunday school, singing in the choir, and too spiritually immature to say no to the desire of my flesh. Consequently, I experienced a set back in my life! I found myself married at 18 years of age, which I thought was the best thing to do. Wrong!

There is one thing that I did not do during this fragile time for me. I didn't walk away from my help. There were days that I wanted to wonder away from my purpose, but I was in too deep. Understand me; I had already experienced the power and love of God. I knew if I let go of Him, I would be miserable for the rest of my life. I had no choice. I had to stay with the Lord, and that resulted with me remaining in my process. Please don't be misconceived; it was not easy, but God's love for me brought me back! What appeared to be destruction for me, turned into my destiny!

Chapter Six
"Don't Forget to Remember"

Just think for a few minutes about the goodness of God in your life. Think about His faithfulness and mercy that He has shown you just this month. I am sure that you will agree with me that God is good. Now why is it that we experience the goodness of the Lord and we know without a doubt that God's grace has saved us, spared our lives, healed our bodies and the list goes on and on, and then we find ourselves in a state of spiritual amnesia? This is definitely not a day to forget God.

This is a day to go after God as never before. As I recall my former life, I celebrate my deliverance. I realize that the love of God rescued me from an existence of degradation and shame. His love brought me back from the dead, and when we are honest with ourselves, we will acknowledge this truth that only God could know me and still love me. While we were yet sinners Christ died for us. Wow! The love that He has for us is unbelievable. How can we forget? Let me answer that. We forget; when we forget to praise Him for what He has already done. Always remember this: our God lives in <u>praise</u>.

> "But thou art holy, O thou that inhabitest the praises of Israel."
>
> *(Psalm 22:1)*

We forget; when we don't pray and are not in constant prayer.

> *"Pray without ceasing."*
>
> *(I Thessalonians 5:17)*

We forget; when we don't devote time in His presence.

> *"Thou wilt shew me the path of life: in thy presence is fullness of joy; at thy right hand there are pleasure for evermore."*
>
> *(Psalm 16:11)*

If we would only remember, then we could perceive the value of the process. David realized the importance of refreshing one's memory of the goodness of God. He was aware that it was God's faithfulness that fortified him, enabling him to stay on his course that God had prepared for him. There was something significant about David.

> *"And when he had removed him, he raised up unto them David to be their king; to whom also he gave testimony, and said, I HAVE FOUND DAVID the son of Jesse, A MAN AFTER MINE OWN HEART, which shall fulfill all my will."*
>
> *(Acts 13:22)*

He had a heart for God which denotes his tenacity to endure until the end. When one has a heart after God, there is a desire to be in His presence and to submit totally to His word. When my heart is in the right place it is virtually impossible for me to forget His kindness that He has shown me. The point that I'm trying to make, is the only way that you and I can keep praising

In The Process

God in the process is to never forget what He's done. Seeing that He will never change, we can expect Him to do more.

David talked about being rescued from a horrible pit. –

> *"He brought me up also out of an horrible pit, out of the miry clay, and set my feet upon a rock, and established my goings."*
>
> *(Psalms 40:2)*

We all have had a pit experience and God brought us out. While we are in, we make promises that we will never forget. "Lord if you bring me out I will serve you for the rest of my life, just get me out of this pit!" Sometimes it feels like the devil had a special meeting in hell, an attack uniquely designed to take me out; and of course, what do I do? Go to God in prayer knowing that I didn't do everything right. Maybe I said the wrong thing or had an attitude. Whatever I did it was wrong and all that I know is that I must get out of this abyss. God our father being the merciful, loving, faithful God that He is, extends His hand, lifts me up and presents to me another opportunity try again. This time I'll try it His way. Now if you consider this scenario, I'll be the first to say that I've revisited this pit cycle more than once and every time God was there to meet me at the point of my need. When I think about it, some crazy undocumented events took place during every cycle and I'm still alive and sane to tell you about it. Now I know that it's personal but not to mention that you're still blessed and have a mind to read my praise report! How can we ever forget? No way possible!

As you walk into your manifestation and receive miracles and breakthroughs from the Lord, be mindful of the one responsible. The faithful God of Covenant always keeps His promises! Now it's time for us to keep ours. Don't forget to remember where all of your blessings come from.

IN THE PROCESS

Chapter Seven
"Pressure"

Some of us live a life that is running over with responsibility. I'll list a few of the hats that I wear: Pastor's Wife, Mother, Grandmother, Evangelist, Teacher, Sister, Mentor, and the list goes on and on. I'm sure you have a list similar to mine and it can become a bit overwhelming at times, but we can not allow our responsibilities to escort us out of the process. Can I be honest? The solution for us is <u>prayer</u>. Don't you think God knows what you're dealing with?

It seems as if we find it difficult to give everything to the Lord and I mean literally everything! As long as we hold on to bits and pieces of the problems, we will always feel the burden involved. Let's examine Paul's solution for this.

> *"Be careful for nothing; but in every thing by prayer and supplication with thanksgiving let your requests be made known unto God. And the peace of God, which passeth all understanding, shall keep your hearts and minds through Christ Jesus."*
> *(Philippians 4:6, 7)*

If we allow God, He will give us the peace that will sustain us during the pressure. Now this peace is not quiet; it's not a 'Calgon take me away' kind of peace, this is a Shalom peace –

nothing missing, nothing broken peace. God desires for us to operate within the encumbering situation as if it weren't there.

God is faithful who will not suffer you to be tempted above that ye are able; but will with the temptation also make a way to escape that ye may be able to bear it. – *(I Corinthians 10:1)* He will give you the strength and tenacity to wear all of your hats and not crumble under the pressure. The pressure in your process is making you great. Now I know you may not agree with me right now, but that's okay. Just agree with God's word.

[handwritten: This is the scripture God gave me in my sleep!]

"It is good for me that I have been afflicted; that I might learn thy statutes."

(Psalms 119:71)

[handwritten: WOW!]

Being in ministry and dealing with people has enabled me to know first hand about pressure, pain, and perseverance. The only thing that helped me continue some days was a life of prayer and my husband, who is my best friend. He is always encouraging me and teaching me how to handle adversity. Let me add this, it is important to be best friends with your spouse. We must submit ourselves to one another and realize with all that you may have going for yourself, you can always learn more. Your spouse should enhance everything you are. When a marriage is united as God desires, adversity will only make the relationship stronger. Don't allow the tension to cause division in your home, but rather use the pressure as a force to propel you into your future. Let's consider Esther. She knew first hand about being in a pressured situation. Esther used

In The Process

her adversity to her advantage; she consecrated herself unto God:

> *"Go, gather together all the Jews that are present in Shushan, and fast ye for me, and neither eat nor drink three days, night or day: I also and my maidens will fast likewise; and so will I go in unto the king, which is not according to the law: and if I perish, I perish."*
>
> *(Esther 4:16)*

Esther was aware that what she was doing was totally unethical. She knew that going before the king unannounced could cost her life, but she realized that the Jews survival was based on her decision to trust God. If we depend on God to meet our need regardless of what we encounter, the pressure will be there, but we won'' feel the weight of it. I can hear the saints of old singing, "Jesus on the main line, tell Him what you want". You probably won't hear the song at your worship service on Sunday, but it is true. It is that easy. He's there for us to communicate with Him. Consider your pressure and inform your pressure about you God. It works, trust me. Think about it. Is there anything hard for God?

Listen, don't crack under pressure, clap under pressure; clap you hands because this is a sign of victory!

> *"Ah Lord God! Behold, thou hast made the heaven and the earth by thy great power and stretched out arm,* **and there is nothing too hard for thee;"**
>
> *(Jeremiah 32:17)*

When you praise God and everything around you says stress, burden, and encumbrance; at this point, you are releasing faith. We know that this absolutely pleases God.

> *"But without faith it is impossible to please him: for he that cometh to God must believe that he is, and that he is a rewarder of them that diligently seek him."*
>
> *(Hebrews 11:6)*

Praise is prophetic in nature because it is dictating to the pressure in your life, "You are only here for a time and there is no power in your attack, you are simply a shadow!" Consequently, what begins to happen is this; God begins to tabernacle with you.

> *"But you are holy, O thou that inhabitest the praises of Israel."*
>
> *(Psalms 22:3)*

You see yourself connected with the Father's predetermined destiny for your life. You know that the enemy's plan is undermined. That's when you will act on pressure with celebration and expectation, allowing it to take you to the next level of glory. Sometimes praise is a sacrifice; so bring it on!

Chapter Eight
"Don't Stop Dreaming"

Have you ever had a desire burning in you and no matter how you tried to ignore this aspiration, it would not go away? Then you ask yourself is this God's desire? If your answer is yes, you are not alone. When you are one with the Lord the more that you grow in Him you are being conformed to His image. The longer I walk with Him and the more intimate I become with Him, His desire becomes my desire. Let's see what the Prophet Amos tells us:

> *"Hate the evil, and love the good, and establish judgment in the gate: it may be that the Lord God of hosts will be gracious unto the remnant of Joseph."*
> *(Amos 5:15)*

This word indicates that we should love what God loves and hate what He hates and when we find ourselves doing that we will receive the desires of our hearts. Remember, He placed the dream there and that is why there is no rest for us until we yield to His process. He works with our decisions when we decide to relinquish our agenda, and that's when he begins to work out His will in us. This is a truth that we must possess. So often we have a strong desire on the inside, but if we don't know that it's God given and, if we don't understand that God honors His word we will allow outside forces, (distractions), to kill our dreams.

I never imaged myself being an author, but God did. The Lord spoke to me through a man of God by the name of Prophet Donald Coleman. He came to one of our worship services. He said, "The Lord says there's a book in you, and the 'body of Christ' needs to read what you have in you". Prior to that night I never gave it any thought. It seemed as if every time we would go to minister there was always a word for us. Please don't get me wrong, I do not despise prophecy. I fully believe that God can and will speak to His people by His spirit, but during this particular time in my life I was fighting a flesh parade. I didn't really understand what it meant to wait on the Lord and I was learning how to trust the Lord. I was very impatient and extremely tired of the same routine everyday. Have you ever experienced a time like this in your life? A time when you've said, I want it and I want it now! God used this man in such a powerful manner that I had no doubt in my mind that it was God. I was <u>instantly</u> encouraged and edified in my spirit.

> *"But he that prophesieth speaketh unto men to edification, and exhortation, and comfort."*
> *(I Corinthians 14:3)*

Get rid of all of those excuses and go after your promise. You're not too old, too short, too tall, too skinny, too fat; you know all of those explanations and inadequacies that we hold on to and allow them to stop us from achieving our goals. You must let them go or the dream in you will never come forth.

In The Process

There were days that I would find myself writing and writing when I didn't know exactly what direction to take. I just continued to write and I found that the key to seeing the process turn into the promise is consistency. This is a powerful word and it is more powerful when put into action! When we become consistent in the process, we can not be moved, and we become like the tree that the psalmist talked about in Psalms 1:3:

> *"And he shall be like a tree planted by the rivers of water, that bringeth forth his fruit in his season; his leaf also shall not wither; and whatsoever he doeth shall prosper."*

This tree had deep roots and a storm, drought, or adverse weather conditions could not move this tree. The roots were strong no matter what the outward appearance looked like. Deep down there was growth, depth, and strength there. This truth applies to a dreamer when the dream is in you and it is something that you must fulfill. If you don't find yourself moving in that direction there will be absolutely no relief for you.

The way your roots become deep is through your consistency; holding to the same principles or practice. This simply means that you are constant; not changing. Maybe you don't feel like pursuing today, but because you are a consistent dreamer, you go after your dream regardless of your feelings. If you remain steadfast in your pursuit you will blossom in your season. That's why you can't stop dreaming now because you have a season, you have a due time and if you humble yourself before Him, He will exalt you in due time! There is greatness in you, and you have a right to dream. Consider this: sometimes you may find yourself dreaming and you say to yourself, "Let me just stop, that could never happen for me". Guess what? Yes it can, and God wants to give you that dream and then some!

> *"Now unto him that is able to do exceeding abundantly above all that we ask or think, according to the power that worketh in us."*
>
> *(Ephesians 3:20)*

A real dreamer will survive in an uncultivated, uninhabited region. That's what we call the wilderness. During this time in your life when God is silent, you don't hear anything in your spirit, no one has given you a word from the Lord, and there is nothing in sight that looks like God. You will continue to visualize yourself living in your destiny. Your dream can not die in the wilderness. Actually, because you know that the dream in you is driven by God, you have to celebrate during this time! You see, this is a period of trusting God and preparation. During this season we have to remain prayerful and <u>stable</u>, firm fixed and lasting. This is what we term "Waiting on the Lord", which is really not a time to sit around and do nothing, but it is a time to gain strength. What does Isaiah tell us to do while waiting?

> *"But they that wait upon the Lord shall renew their strength; they shall mount up with wings as eagles; they shall run, and not be weary; and they shall walk, and not faint."*

In The Process

(Isaiah 40:31)

We should become like new. We should be soaring! We should find ourselves dreaming with great expectation. If you've stopped dreaming for whatever reason, this is what I want you to do. Pick up where you left off. *insert?

Everything the devil told you that you could never do, God says you can in and through Jesus Christ! You can do **ALL** things through Christ that gives you strength. You are the visionary! It's time to dream again!

In the Process

Chapter Nine
"Friends"

"A person whom one knows well and is fond of; companion, confidant, a supporter. A friend loveth at all times..."

(Proverbs 17:17)

I would always hear my grandmother say, "Friends, if you get one in this life, you did good." Not to mention, a best friend. I believe that a friend is one that you don't have to see everyday, but you know that the individual is always there to support you. I don't mean condone your wrong decisions or bad behavior, but because they love you, they will tell you when you are wrong without thinking twice, and still love you.

A true friend has a commitment and loyalty to the relationship. You will find in your process that there will be those who will say, "I'm your friend", but what they display will be the total opposite. This should not be taken lightly considering that anyone that we call friend, usually are allowed speak into our lives. They talk and we listen. When you develop a relationship with someone, male or female, you must be sure that they have the same mind that you have. Often we think when the word of God tells us <u>not</u> to be unequally yoked together with unbelievers that it's a directive given to individuals preparing for marriage. Not so!

> *"Be ye not unequally yoked together with unbelievers: for what fellowship hath righteousness with unrighteousness? And what communion hath light with darkness?"*
>
> *(II Corinthians 6:14)*

It means exactly what it says and that applies to everyone that is a believer. We cannot mix what we believe with the world's ideology. We cannot compromise or let our standards down because we feel lonely and need a friend. There will be times in your life that you will look around you and no one will be there. I recall when I would say, "I don't have any friends. I can't call anyone to go shopping with me or have coffee with me, what's wrong?" Then I realized nothing was wrong, I needed a lesson in being alone with God. Now understand you can make this learning experience a pleasant one or it can become a nightmare for you. My advice to you is just submit to this lesson and you will begin to see that you're not alone. This is an occasion to be still and know that He is God!

> *"Be still, and know that I am God: I will be exalted among the heathen, I will be exalted in the earth."*
>
> *(Psalms 46:10)*

When God begins to speak a word to us it is a specific word for your purpose and process. Therefore, I may not understand what He's saying to you, which explains why our friends don't always get excited when we share with them what the Lord is saying to us. It's not always a case of my friend is a hater. Possibly, they just didn't receive it like you

In The Process

did, because it's not for them. Sometimes you have to be like Mary the mother of Jesus. She knew the babe wrapped in swaddling clothes was Christ the Anointed one, but she considered the revelation carefully within her heart.

> *"But Mary kept all these things, and pondered them in her heart."*
>
> *(Luke 2:19)*

Let me add this: Please be certain that you are not deserted, because you're not amicable. That's why it is imperative that we live life free from the negative after-math; (issues). We have had many collisions in life, which have been the root cause of our isolation. Perhaps you have encountered rejection in a relationship with someone that promised to be a friend for life and had a change of mind at some point. These disappointments result in great heartache, and this is an ache that only God can heal! God promised us a life free from hurt and pain and a major procedure in this process is allowing our God to mend our broken hearts. Right now is the perfect time to allow Him to come into your heart and love away the wounds and the scars from your past.

One of our working definitions for friend is a supporter. I find this synonym instrumental in understanding the characteristics of a true friend. If one calls themselves your confidant; they will support you when they understand or when they don't. Our greatest example of a friend is our Lord Jesus Christ. He showed us that a friend is there at all times, closer than a biological brother, and that friend, will consider your situation before himself. He gave His life; what a friend we

Lisa C. Brooks

have in Jesus!

> *"Greater love hath no man than this, that a man lay down his life for his friends. Ye are my friends, if ye do whatsoever I command you."*
>
> *(John 15:13,14)*

This scripture reveals to us that we are His friends if we walk in His love and obey His word. He expects us to act like a friend to Him. *(Selah)* Before we move on, let's get one thing clear. If you say that you and God are friends, then you're telling me that you made the choice to forsake the world and sell-out totally to Him? This is the wisest decision that one could make. Our God is very territorial, and He wants all or nothing at all. He's a jealous God.

> *"For the Lord thy God is a consuming fire, even a jealous God."*
>
> *(Deuteronomy 4:24)*

"Best Friends"

If you are married, then your best friend should be your spouse! We know that our Heavenly Father is our best friend. We can talk to the Lord and we don't have to worry

In The Process

about hearing any of our secrets later. That's exactly what we should be experiencing in our marriage relationship. There should be no hesitation concerning communicating with your spouse, and there definitely should be **no** secret's. Pastor Brooks loves to talk, and he wants you to engage in conversation. I'm talking about a two hour conversation. We have lunch together everyday; that's our special time. I love it when he talks to me and he asks me, "You follow me"? I find myself more excited everyday at lunch time. We bond more and more as the years go by. You know what? You can have a honeymoon experience whenever you choose to.

This display of love, loyalty, commitment, and unity in holy matrimony is God's idea. Let me prove it.

> *"For this cause shall a man leave his father and mother, and shall be joined unto his wife, and they two shall be one flesh. This is a great mystery, but I speak concerning Christ and the church."*
>
> (Ephesians 5:31, 32)

I agree with Paul. This is truly a mystery. There are commandments throughout the word of God that we may never understand. As we obey His word the result of our willingness to carry out the orders, there is always blessings and favor.

God's plan for marriage is equivalent to Christ and the church, His body, His bride. He's the bridegroom and we will always find Him in control and the head of the church. He will always love the body, and nurture the body. The body is protected and covered because we are one with Him; no division. He knows what we are in need of. He has freely given to us all things, to enjoy. He wants us to be happy and prosperous. What a bridegroom!

That is what our relationship should be like with our spouses; our best friends. Now, I know you maybe saying within yourself right now, "That's wishful thinking, and it's not possible". Sorry my friend it is possible. If it weren't attainable, it wouldn't be in the word of God. If we submit ourselves to the will of God and to one another we will have a marriage that represents Christ and His bride, (the Body of Christ). No doubt your best friend will get under your skin, and there will be times when you won't feel like looking, talking, sharing, or touching; but it's okay! That's when you go to your best, best friend and ask Him for the grace and strength to deal with your best friend. We all have a process and we all have a process. We all have a responsibility to uphold one another and love our best friends. Not just in word, but in our deeds.

Understand our adversary the devil hates marriage, unity, and love and He's going to attempt; *(notice I used the word attempt)*, to destroy the institution of marriage. So if we know this, we have a God-given mandate given responsibility to stop this attack; and it starts with us. We must be committed to the things of God and then we can pull the curtain down on the divorce court in the Body of Christ. We must do more than believe God for our mates. It's time to love on them, talk to them, listen to them, be patient with them, and support their process and purpose. This is when you will become the finest friend a spouse can have. It may be a little struggle for you at first, but remember, submit to God first, and you will find the other steps easy to take. Go ahead! Your best friend is waiting for you!

Chapter Ten
"Family"

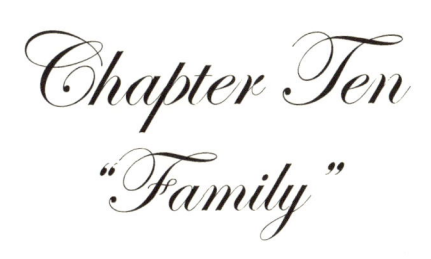

Family – (defined): Household, parents and their children, relatives, all those descended from a common ancestor, lineage, a group of similar or related things.

At the launch of this writing I was hesitant concerning family and close friends. I mean, I wanted to share my process with the world to encourage someone to continue with the Lord. At the same time understanding that it might involve someone else's process to get my point across.

When you consider family, there are so many thoughts that come to mind. Family should represent a relationship that exhibits trust, loyalty, unity, and love; just to name a few. There are times when we do not experience the joy of the ideal family and we encounter just the opposite. There are situations that arise in life when the last thing that you want to deal with is a love one or someone close to you applying insult to the injury that you are confronted with. I've learned in the process that focus is everything. God poke to Abraham in Genesis 12:1-2:

"NOW THE Lord had said unto Abram, Get thee out

of thy country, and from thy kindred, and from thy father's house, unto a land that I will show thee: And I will make of thee a great nation, and I will bless thee, and make thy man great; and thou shalt be a blessing."

Abraham's obedience to the command of the Lord was the beginning of His purpose being manifested the directive that He was so significant seeing that nothing could happen for him until he separated himself from his ancestry. We must operate in the same manner as Abraham, we must see God's plan for our lives as the number one priority in life. We need to forsake all to do so! Now this does not insinuate that we neglect our children and our responsibility to love and pray for our loved ones, but we cannot allow anything or anyone to come before our obligation to the things of God. Of course, situations will occur concerning our family members that will weigh heavy on our hearts, but that's when we must find ourselves making our requests known to our God. He is Father of us all. Therefore, He is more concerned about your loved ones than you are. They really belong to Him anyway, and since He gives us time on earth to enjoy a relationship with them; we cannot forget this is only temporary. We cannot live through our children, and neither can we make any of our descendants say yes to the Lord. They have been given free will just as you and I have and choosing life is ultimately their decision.

It was so important for me to share this information with you, because so often we are consumed with being validated

In The Process

by our family members. So much so, until we loose sight of the one that really matters. Family is God's idea. He desires for His people to have "Zoë; the God-kind" of relationships with their families. God does not desire for His people to place any family member before Him. The biological family should be valuable to us. In contrast, the spiritual family; (the body of Christ), should be as significant, if not more so than our natural families. We are connected in the spirit with an obligation to one another! God informs us in His word that there is no relationship with Him that excludes your brothers and sisters in the Lord. We must love one another.

> *"If a man say, I love God, and hateth his brother, he is a liar; for he that loveth not his brother whom he hath seen, how can he love God whom he hath not seen?"*
>
> *(I John 4:20)*

We should feel the necessity to uphold one another. That may require loving and supporting a total stranger. God tells us that we are fitly joined together. Therefore, it doesn't matter if I know you or not, I still have to love you. I know some of you are reading this book and saying to yourselves, or to someone else, "She must be crazy, my feelings have been hurt, I've been lied on, betrayed, and abandoned by a loved one". Listen, I know it hurts, but guess what? What you feel is real, but you can't allow your feelings to dictate your response to the word of God! Our God is a God of love and mercy. That is why the process is so vital. As we continue to mature in the things of God, we will begin to find ourselves loving one another without a struggle.

Do not concentrate on how many times that you have been mistreated by someone close to you, but rather give attention to what the word of the Lord promises us when we give up all to follow Him.

> *"And Jesus answered and said, Verily I say unto you, There is no man that hath left house, or brethren, or sisters, or father, or mother, or wife, or children, or lands, for my sake, and the gospel's."*
>
> *(Mark 10:29)*

I want you to take inventory of all of your family members that you communicate with on a regular basis. Whether they're biological or spiritual family; and then make sure that they are on the same page with you. It should be God first, and everything else secondary! Now if you find some one on your list that is not on your page, there is a problem, and you may have to do a *Genesis 12:1 - "Get thee out of thy country, and from thy kindred, . . . unto a land that I will show thee."*

This stage in life may be a little lonely, but it's okay; because of the greater the sacrifice, the greater the glory! Never allow anyone to disrespect the God in you. There might have pressure applied to your character to compromise, but if you stand your ground, represent Jesus, you will not regret it!

Don't be surprised if you find yourself helping that relative that has caused you the most grief. The one that you said you'd love from a distance and just pray for them. Yea, that's the one that you will feel compelled to rescue out of their stupor! That's just like God isn't it? Well we know that

In The Process

God is love, and His love is shed abroad in our hearts by His spirit. As a result, we must love one another. That love must be displayed to those that aren't easy to love. It might appear to be unfair, but it's rewarding, considering families are being obliterated everyday. It's time for restoration to take place in our families! Now that's spiritual warfare.

"They are so precious..."

When Pastor Brooks and I married, this was one of the most exciting days of my life. Of course, nothing compares to the day that I received the Lord as Savior of my life. I was honored to become Mrs. Michael A. Brooks. We were friends for many years and it was amazing to me how things transpired over time. I was most impressed by his love for God and his principles he had for the institution of family. I always noticed his concern, for his children. Regardless of various tumultuous attacks on his character, he never neglected his responsibility as father.

Let me explain, we have a blended family, and in case you're wondering, yes it was an adjustment. He had two children; a girl and a boy, and I had three girls. I remember the day before we were leaving for our honeymoon to Cancun, Mexico. We took all of the children to lunch and made the big announcement. It felt as if the earth stood still. There was total silence and they began to stare in each others eyes for about five minutes. Next they began to look at my husband, and I as if to say, you're my stepmother, and you are my stepfather? My heart was beating rapidly, and I just wanted someone to say something. Please, just break the silence! Finally, someone said, "Can we order now?"

Now back to the adjustment segment. We have a commanding responsibility from God to raise our children in the fear of the Lord.

> *"And ye fathers provoke not your children to wrath: but bring them up in the nurture and admonition of the Lord."*
>
> *(Ephesians 6:4)*

If we obey God's word concerning our children, we will see the fruit of it as they mature and become adults. There are times when we look at our children and think what a sweet, innocent loving child, but that little one needs Jesus and we cannot sanction our children to rule our household. They are not to operate as the priest of the family. The priest of the family is defined as the male father who is present in the home, or the female who is in position as single parent. You are the priest of your home, you make the decisions, YOU provide for your family; NOT the child. Our children are precious and they are a blessing from God, but they will run right over you if you permit them to. You must keep them in their place.

Love is necessary, but so is correction. I know it may be difficult to enforce it, but it's better for you to display the chastisement than a stranger that has absolutely no regard for your child. We are the children of God and those that He loves He chastens.

> *"For whom the Lord loveth He chasteneth, and scourgeth every son whom he receiveth."*
> *(Hebrews 12:6)*

I'll conclude by saying this: If we apply the proper discipline now, we will see the fruit of it later.

> *"Correct thy son, and he shall give thee rest; yea, he shall give delight unto thy soul."*
> *(Proverbs 29:17)*

Now let me encourage you. If you are dealing with a son or daughter that you have raised and you know without a doubt you have them in the Lord; and your Christian example has been of good quality; then you are not responsible for their decisions. Now they are adult and they have to choose life just as you and I did. This can be a very crucial time in your process, because you cannot authorize your offspring to interrupt your life.

Therefore, be cognizant of this; we all belong to God and that includes your children. Yes, you love them, but remember there's someone who loves them more than you can ever imagine.

Chapter Eleven
"I Got This!"

Being in control is a natural occurrence for the human being. Out of this drive to be in charge, it can get us into trouble. If we don't live life as God being the head of our lives, we are simply wasting time; because that's the way He planned it. We were created to trust Him. He absolutely loves it when we rest in Him, seeing that this rest is indicative of one acknowledging who He is. We deal with so much grief and agony when we don't allow Him to be the Lord of our lives.

There is only one way that we can live in this rest and trust. We must learn of Him. Who He is? What is He capable of? We have to understand Him and learn His method as well as adopt His thinking! Someone may be asking, "Why is this necessary and how can this be done?" I'm glad you asked.

The prophet Isaiah tells us to stop trusting in man.

> *"Stop trusting in man, who has but a breath in his nostrils of what account is he?"*
> *(Isaiah 2:22 – NIV)*

This subject of trust was weighing heavily on my heart, and when I thought I was finished writing, I found it necessary to share my thoughts with you on this matter. If we don't trust the Lord we will never walk in His promises. I'm reminded of the instructions that He gave Moses for the children of Israel:

> *"Be careful to follow every command I am giving you today, so that you may live and increase and may enter and possess the land that the Lord promised on oath to your forefathers."*
>
> *(Deuteronomy 8:1 NIV)*

You may say what does obedience have to do with trust? Everything! If I take the Lord at His word before possession takes place, I'm showing the Lord by faith, (trust, and confidence in God's word), that I'm expecting every promise to be performed!

I've learned that my obedience to the word of God causes me to live life in the blessings of God. Let's examine the word **obey**: *to carry out the orders, submit, surrender, or yield.* If I trust the Lord, then it will never be a problem with me carrying out His orders; because I know from past experiences what He's capable of doing. Our God always reveals Himself, or should I say, shows His power to those that reverence Him!

> *"The Lord confides in those who fear Him; He makes His covenant known to them."*
>
> *(Psalms 25:14 – NIV)*

It is so moving to know that God will **not** keep us in the dark concerning His plan and His heart for us; but this privilege only comes with trust. My heart began to rejoice when I realized that I have an attorney that I can trust and He's never lost a case! Yes, I know that sounds a little old fashion, but think about it; it's true. I John 2:1 talks about our advocate, a counselor: one who can do something for you that you can't do for yourself.

> *"My little children, these things write I unto you, that ye sin not. And if any man sin, we have an advocate with the Father Jesus Christ the righteous."*
> *(I John 2:1)*

This word does not give us a license to sin, but if we do we have Jesus, our very present help, to lift us up and give us a new "Yes Lord". My point is this; if you have a defense attorney that cannot be defeated, why try to defend *(to act as lawyer for – vindicate, protect, justify, uphold)*, yourself? I'm sure you've heard the term, "I got this". Well, this is a term that every believer needs to loose! There is a God that is powerful and in control, and if we only trust Him to be who He is, we will find out that He's the undisputed *champion of the world* and everything in it! He had this under control before we got here. Therefore my friend, there's no need for us to attempt to assist Him! Now, He doesn't need our help, and besides, do you really want to prolong your process?

Chapter Twelve
"May I Help You?"

"Even as the Son of man came not to be ministered unto, but to minister, and to give his life a ransom for many."

(Matthew3 20:28)

Come go with me to the 1979. I'm sure that you can remember a few specific events that took place in your life that had a great impact in your decisions and your future. I want to share my experience in what I call my "ministry boot camp". I was 15 years old in the kitchen of a Pentecostal church that I had been a member of for 15 years. My drill sergeants were the church mothers; and by the way, all of them weren't sweet little nurturing mothers, praying and kissing the kids on the forehead. Actually, some of them were quite the opposite, although believe me I received hands on training that I'll never forget. In this space of time, which I refer to as my preparation period, I leaned how to serve dinners for the church anniversary, while working with the children; and teaching their Sunday school class. I was faithfully on my post on 'youth day'; with my crisp white blouse, my black skirt, as I stood at the door with a big smile, ushering people to their seats. In all of this, something was missing. The ingredient

I lacked was understanding the revelation of the ministry of helps.

> *"And god hath set some in the church, first apostles, secondarily prophets, thirdly teachers, after that miracles, then gifts of healings, helps, governments, diversities of tongues."*
>
> *(I Corinthians 12:28)*

There is absolutely no way that I can share my declaration of restoration with you and omit to include my maturation process in ministry. I'm not referring to the stage that we consider the pulpit ministry; I'm interested in the real meaning of ministry. Let's examine Webster's definition for minister: A servant one authorized to conduct religious services in a church, to give help. Without making things difficult, I must explain the Greek definition for minister, which is of the essence for us because it gives us the true meaning of what God defines as a minister in His word.

Diakonos – A servant, attendant, to wait upon.

Now the next time someone tells you that they have been called to ministry, you should witness them serving and attending to the needs of their spiritual covering. This includes serving the people of God. Understand this is not an area of competition or show of intellectual ability. Ministry is a territory of humility. If I had only two words to choose from that describe ministry, those words would be: *sacrifice and life*. My first choice; **sacrifice**: which is to give up, let go, yield, or

In The Process

relinquish, is a concise description of what is required of us as ministers. We are living sacrifices.

> *"I beseech you therefore, brethren, by the mercies of God, that ye present your bodies a living sacrifice, holy acceptable unto God, which is your reasonable service."*
>
> *(Romans 12:1)*

This sacrifice is not for you; it's for someone else! Ouch! It's a matter of the heart and we must perceive ourselves as God's representatives. This simply indicates that I must say and do what He would say or do. Actually a minister has a responsibility to live a life worthy of the call and to glorify God in all things.

> *". . . if any man minister, let him do it as of the ability which God giveth. . ."*
>
> *(I Peter 4:11)*

As we comprehend this revelation of ministry, we understand that it's not about cards, capes, and briefcases, but it's about <u>serving</u>. When you first begin to yield your will and your agenda to God's program for your life, you will find it a bit uncomfortable. Yet, with each passing day it will become a joyful experience in your process. Let's deal with Jesus' attitude about sacrifice.

> *"Looking unto Jesus the author and finisher of our faith; who for the joy that was set before him endured the cross, despising the shame, and is set down at the*

> *right hand of the throne of God."*
>
> *(Hebrews 12:2)*

The writer tells us to look to Jesus! Keep your thoughts and focus on Him! When you start feeling like you are not appreciated and no one cares, just keep serving and consider your example. We must serve Him first and follow His lead. This involves a death of the flesh.

Right here is where my second choice of words come in; **life.** That's what we lose when we are ministers for the Lord. You lose your life.

> *"He that loveth his life shall lose it; and he that hateth his life in this world shall keep it unto life eternal. If any man serve me, let him follow me; and where I am, there shall also my servant be: if any man serve me, him will my Father honour."*
>
> *(John 12:25, 26)*

You don't have a life. Paul said, "My life is his with Christ in God." This says that I should never see "me" in action, instead I should always acknowledge who called me and where my strength comes from. Consequently, the Lord empowers us to serve. That power within us is for His people, and it's not for us to sit back like the super saint!

> *"The Spirit of the Lord is upon me, because he hath anointed me to preach the Gospel to the poor; he hath sent me to heal the brokenhearted, to preach deliverance to the captives, and recovering of sight to the blind, to set at liberty them that are bruised. To*

In The Process

preach the acceptable year of the Lord."
(Luke 4:18, 19)

Please don't misunderstand this truth. He is the <u>wonder</u>, not us. Our heavenly Father loved us so much that He gave us the very best that He could offer. If we call to mind what the Lord endured, so you and I could be free, then we can consider what we sacrifice on a daily basis as nothing! Yes, I said nothing! There is no comparison to what He sacrificed. You see, we may have to go out of our way to help someone. That may call us out of our <u>comfort</u> zone. You know what I'm saying; we have a zone, that is convenient; "for me, my schedule, and my time". It's okay as long as I don't have to come out of my zone. Let me ask you a question. Has anyone spit in your face because you are a disciple? Have you shed any blood? Have you been beaten for the sake of Christ? The majority of us would answer no.

"For consider him that endured such contradiction of sinners against himself, lest ye be wearied and faint in your minds. Ye have not yet resisted unto blood, striving against sin."
(Hebrews 12:3, 4)

Therefore, all complaining should cease and more submission should take place. The only way that we can serve effectively is to keep our hearts covered by the word of God. I mentioned to you that it is a matter of the heart. If our hearts aren't lined up with the word of God we will never serve. You may think no one knows me! Guess what? You don't even know you, so

Lisa C. Brooks

please don't trust yourself. No one will ever know you like the one that made you.

> *"The heart is deceitful above all things, and desperately wicked: who can know it? And it shall come to pass, when thou shalt show this people all these words, and they shall say unto thee. Wherefore hath the Lord pronounced all this great evil against us? Or what is your iniquity? Or what is our sin that we have committed against the Lord our God?"*
>
> *(Jeremiah 17:9, 10)*

Basically, I want to encourage you to never stop serving. Of course, you will be challenged, your feelings will be hurt, you will be ignored, but remember it's not for you! You man never hear someone call your name and give you a trophy for *minister of the year!* Our ultimate goal is to hear our Lord say, "Well done, thy good and faithful servant". So, whatever you do, keep your goal in front of you. Do everything necessary in this life to reach that goal. Lose sight of you and you'll see the big picture! Your labor is not in vain!

> *"Therefore, my beloved brethren, be ye stedfast, unmoveable, always abounding in the work of the Lord, forasmuch as ye know that your labour is not in vain in the Lord."*
>
> *(I Corinthians 15:58)*

Now, I understand what Paul meant when He said grow in grace and in the wisdom of our Lord. It is only a mature disciple that will conform to servant. Certainly, if we don't mature, it will never make sense and we will always have an excuse not to serve. What if Jesus made an excuse not to go to calvary's cross? Where would we be?

I have been notorious
for abandoning my
dreams!

Asking God to help
me to revisit my
dreams.

What makes me uncomfortable
✱ white people with dreds
2 year old children, speaking full
sentences in diapers

Chapter Thirteen
"Will I Ever Arrive?"

As we have come to the culmination of this writing, I hope that you can look at your process with great appreciation. Don't waste time and days with circumstances and people that don't really matter, but rather pursue your dreams and aspirations until you attain them.

I've disclosed some extremely private episodes that have occurred in my life, with you. All so that you could get an idea of what my journey has been like for the last 40 years. Seeing that you know my view on family, friends, dreams, and ministry; I pray that you may have a better understanding of your perception concerning your process. I found it very difficult to end this book, because it never stops; this continuum of the process that we are in; the growth that we experience, our family and friends that we interact with on a daily basis, and of course the work of the ministry. These are things and people that we will encounter as long as we live. We never arrive to a position of STOP, and if you do, you have problems. When you stop, you don't go forward. Eventually, you will either digress or die spiritually. Don't misunderstand me, we should reach a place of maturity in God where we live as Paul instructed us; *"Forgetting those things which are behind, and reaching forth"*. Even as mature disciples, we will always be in a process in life. Everything that we experience should prepare us for the next stage of faith and glory. That's why it is important to go with, God's flow and stay on course. I mean, isn't it exciting to know that as we stay with the Lord through training and personal participation we will live in His promises. I encourage you to take one day at a time and with each day spend time with Daddy God. It is so important for us to stay before Him and receive complete healing from all of the negative events that have taken place during our lives. I'm talking about the hurt and disappointment you experienced that your adversary thought would cause you to loose your mind, take your life, or take someone else's; but mercy said "NO!"

I want you to make a covenant with me, simply because we need one another and it is always refreshing to know that you're not in this alone, but someone is praying with me and for me. The Lord informed us about the power of agreement.

> *"Again I say unto you, That if two of you shall agree on earth as touching any thing that they shall ask, it shall be done for them of my Father which is in heaven. For where two or three are gathered together in my name, there am I in the midst of them."*
> *(Matthew 18:19,20)*

We have been given authority in Jesus' name and if we don't use what has been given to us, whose fault is it? Exactly. That is why we must unite our hearts and agree to the following:

- Stay in your process
- Water your seed
- Never stop saying – *"Yes Lord"!*

In The Process

➢ Encourage someone else to purchase this book!

Now that we've made covenant, we must follow the example of our Lord. He will never break a vow. I'm depending on you to live your dreams, and you can rely on me to pray for you *in your process*.

IN THE PROCESS

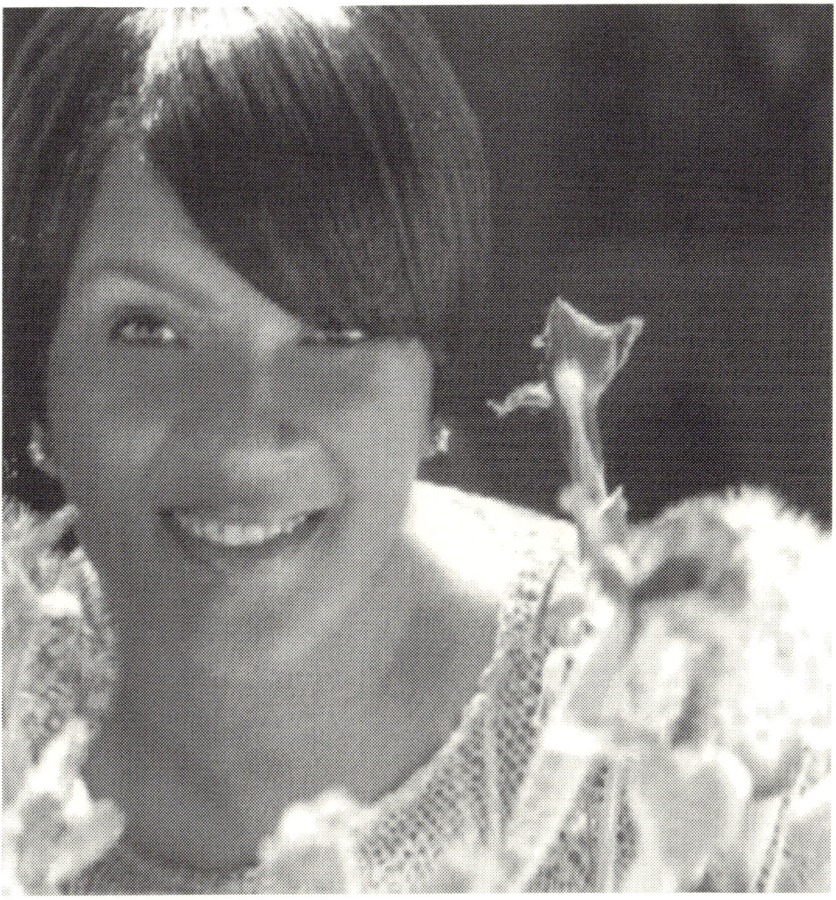

About the Author

Some people are simply born with a destiny and calling. In the first chapter of Jeremiah, God tells the Old Testament prophet: "I knew you before you were born...I sanctified you and appointed you as my spokesman to the world." Lisa Brooks was born to speak to the generation in like manner. She is an anointed psalmist and a powerful preacher and teacher of the gospel.

Lisa serves in pastoral ministry with her husband Michael Brooks. They are the founders of the Restoration Fellowship Church Int'l in Southfield Michigan where she is the director and founder of the ministries' women's group, RWS- Restored Women Sharing. Pastor Lisa remarks, our purpose is simply this: God specializes in meeting individuals at the point of their need, we serve for the express purpose of leading women to that place of surrender where the Holy Spirit can gain access to their spirit to meet their needs both spiritually and emotionally. It is our conviction that the same power that raised Jesus from the dead resurrects broken lives entombed in sin and the graves of social economic deadness. By sharing the word of God we restore one another in the spirit of meekness through the love of Jesus Christ."

As the lead singer of the group "Witness", she delivers a message of hope declaring God's love and his power to deliver those in captivity. Lisa is the recipient of the Stellar Award, Gospel music excellence award, and has been

Lisa C. Brooks

nominated for Dove and Grammy awards as well. Pastor Lisa comments, "We must understand that the accomplishments that God allows us to achieve are only one level of success in him positioning us for the next level. Ministry in every form is very serious for it involves the souls of mankind. Our world needs an encounter with the true and living God and he has called us to be his representatives. At the end of the day I just want to know that in some way, some how I was an agent of change to lead a lost soul into the kingdom of God."

Oh sweet wonder!